D1518885

Inside Animals

Spiders

and Other Creepy–Crawlies

David West

WINDMILL BOOKS

Published in 2018 by **Windmill Books**,
an imprint of Rosen Publishing
29 East 21st Street, New York, NY 10010

Designed and illustrated *by* David West

CATALOGING-IN-PUBLICATION DATA
Names: West, David.
Title: Spiders and other creepy-crawlies / David West.
Description: New York : Windmill Books, 2018. | Series: Inside animals | Includes index.
Identifiers: ISBN 9781508194309 (pbk.) | ISBN 9781508193890 (library bound) |
ISBN 9781508194361 (6 pack)
Subjects: LCSH: Spiders–Juvenile literature. | Insects–Juvenile literature.
Classification: LCC QL467.2 W47 2018 | DDC 595.7–dc23

Manufactured in China
CPSIA Compliance Information: Batch BW18WM: For Further Information contact Rosen Publishing, New York, New York at 1-800-237-9932

Contents

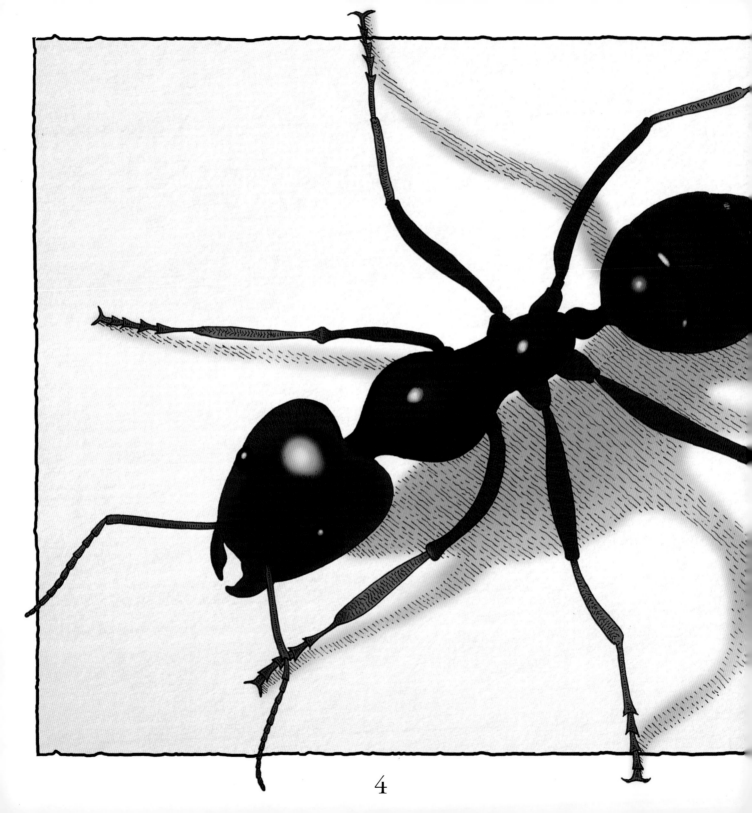

Ant

Ants are insects. They have a hard casing on the outside called an exoskeleton. They have six legs, and their body is made of three parts—head, chest, and abdomen. Ants attack and defend themselves by biting and sometimes by stinging. Ants have large heads with powerful jaws. They can carry 50 times their own body weight.

Ants share their food with the rest of the colony. When they find some food, they leave a special chemical trail back to the nest. Other ants can follow the trail to the food source.

Inside an Ant

Antenna

Two antennae pick up chemical signals. They also tell other ants which colony they are from.

Saliva gland

This is one of many glands that provide liquids to help ants eat and digest food.

Brain

Eye

Pincers

Ants have large muscles in their heads to power their sharp pincers. They use them to carry food and as weapons.

Nerves

Six legs

Ants are insects, and all insects have six legs.

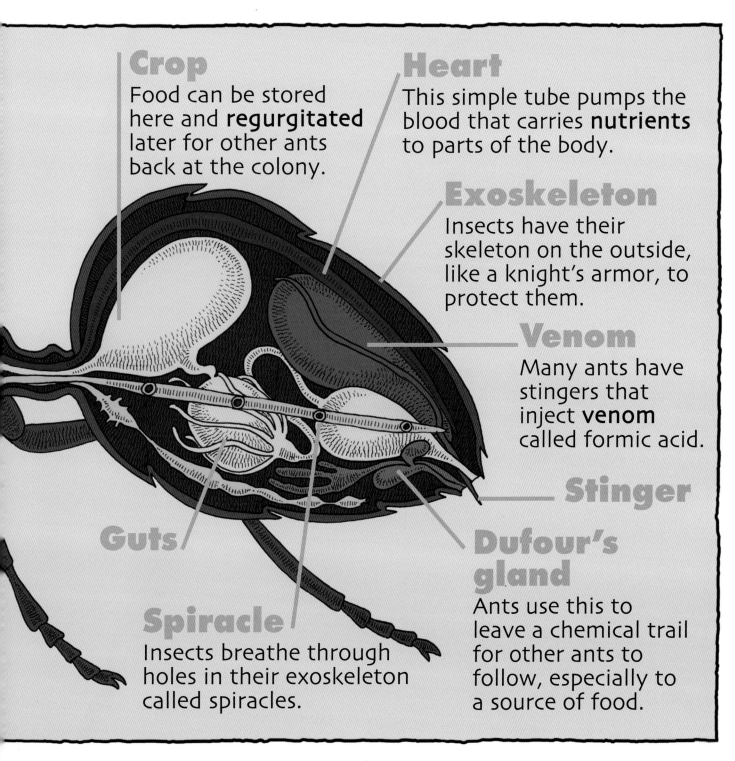

Crop
Food can be stored here and **regurgitated** later for other ants back at the colony.

Heart
This simple tube pumps the blood that carries **nutrients** to parts of the body.

Exoskeleton
Insects have their skeleton on the outside, like a knight's armor, to protect them.

Venom
Many ants have stingers that inject **venom** called formic acid.

Stinger

Dufour's gland
Ants use this to leave a chemical trail for other ants to follow, especially to a source of food.

Guts

Spiracle
Insects breathe through holes in their exoskeleton called spiracles.

Bee

Bees are insects with wings. Like all insects, they have three body parts and an exoskeleton. They collect **nectar** from flowers and turn it into honey. They take the honey back to their hive and feed it to the baby bees, called larvae. Honey bees show other bees where the food is by doing a special movement called a waggle dance.

This is a honey bee. Farmers like honey bees because they collect pollen while they drink nectar. The pollen gets carried to other flowers, helping them to produce seeds and fruit.

Inside a **Bee**

Brain

Eyes
The two main eyes are called compound eyes because they are made up of lots of little eyes.

Antenna
These are used to smell, measure speed of flight, and to communicate with other bees.

Mouth
The tongue laps up nectar. Muscles squeeze the nectar into its mouth and then to its stomachs.

Flying muscles
The strong wing muscles allow the wings to flap up to 200 beats per second.

Exoskeleton

Tongue

Nerves

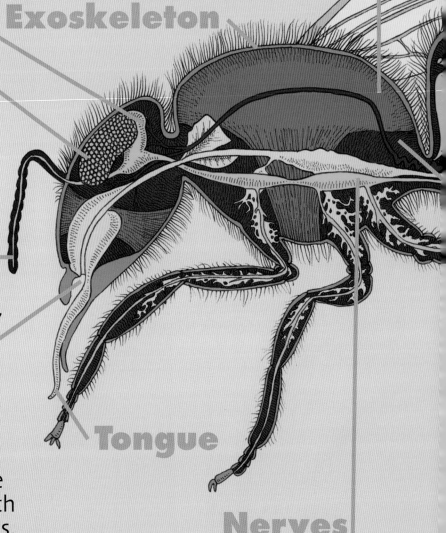

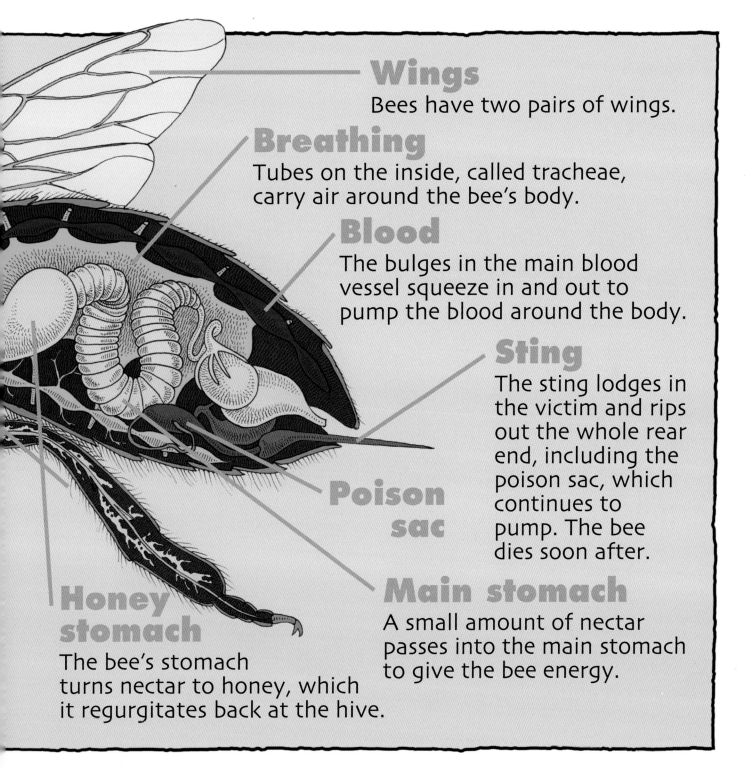

Wings
Bees have two pairs of wings.

Breathing
Tubes on the inside, called tracheae, carry air around the bee's body.

Blood
The bulges in the main blood vessel squeeze in and out to pump the blood around the body.

Sting
The sting lodges in the victim and rips out the whole rear end, including the poison sac, which continues to pump. The bee dies soon after.

Poison sac

Main stomach
A small amount of nectar passes into the main stomach to give the bee energy.

Honey stomach
The bee's stomach turns nectar to honey, which it regurgitates back at the hive.

Mosquito

Mosquitoes are insects that are members of the fly family. They feed on nectar and plant juices, although females feed on blood as well. They inject their thin, needle-like **proboscis** into the skin to find a blood vessel. They search for their victim's hot breath with their antennae. Their wings beat so fast they make a high-pitched buzz.

Mosquitoes inject their saliva into the blood vessel to stop the blood from clogging up. This irritates the skin and leaves a red, itchy spot.

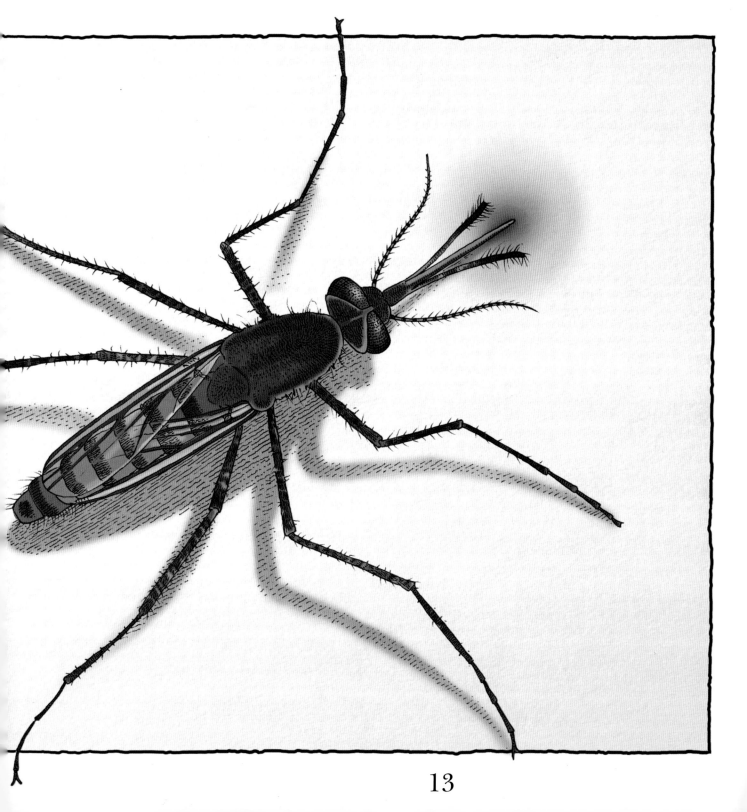

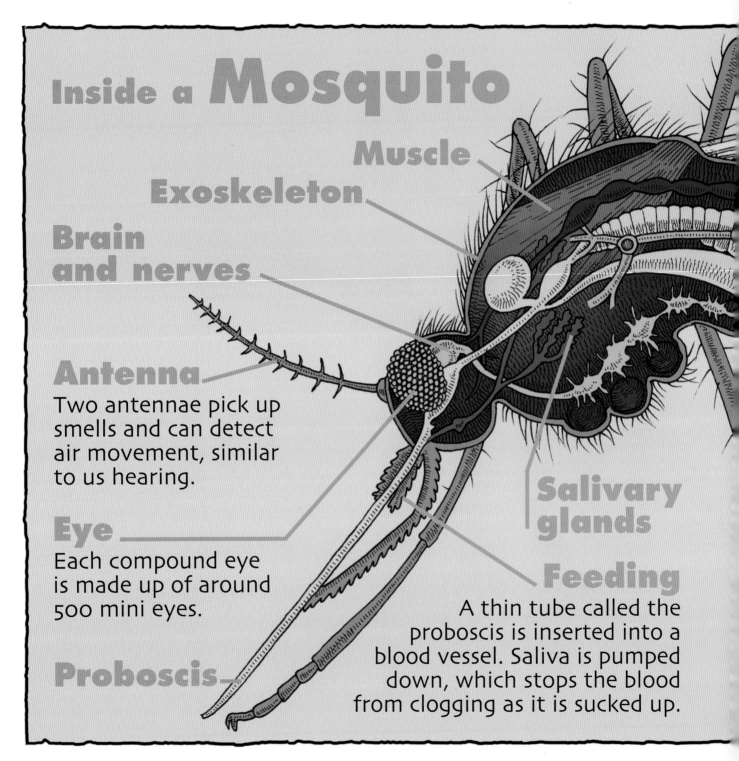

Inside a **Mosquito**

Muscle

Exoskeleton

Brain and nerves

Antenna

Two antennae pick up smells and can detect air movement, similar to us hearing.

Eye

Each compound eye is made up of around 500 mini eyes.

Proboscis

Salivary glands

Feeding

A thin tube called the proboscis is inserted into a blood vessel. Saliva is pumped down, which stops the blood from clogging as it is sucked up.

14

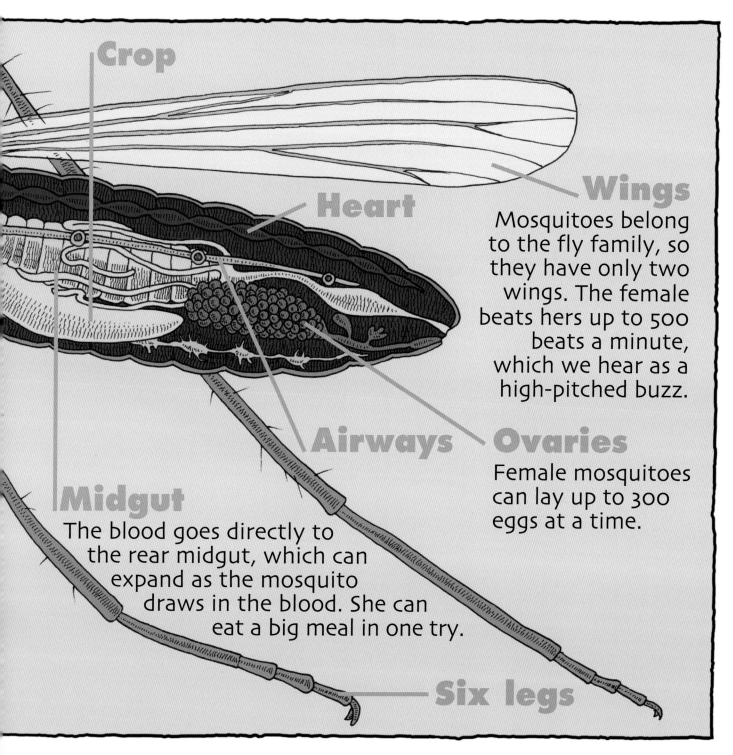

Crop

Heart

Wings

Mosquitoes belong to the fly family, so they have only two wings. The female beats hers up to 500 beats a minute, which we hear as a high-pitched buzz.

Airways

Ovaries

Female mosquitoes can lay up to 300 eggs at a time.

Midgut

The blood goes directly to the rear midgut, which can expand as the mosquito draws in the blood. She can eat a big meal in one try.

Six legs

Spider

Spiders are arachnids. All arachnids have eight legs and a skeleton on the outside called an exoskeleton. Their body has two parts—the head and chest, which are joined together, and an abdomen. All spiders can spin silk, and many make webs to catch insects. They use their fangs to inject poison into their prey.

This hairy tarantula is one of the biggest spiders. Some can grow to the size of a dinner plate. They hunt animals as large as lizards, mice, birds, and small snakes.

Inside a Spider

Brain

Some spiders' brains and nervous systems take up almost 80% of their bodies, even spilling into their legs!

Eyes

Spiders can have up to eight eyes.

Sucking stomach

Prey is broken down into fluid, and the juices are sucked up by the stomach.

Venom gland

Fangs

Spiders inject their prey with venom to kill it.

Legs

Spiders, like all arachnids, have eight legs.

Midgut

Spiders have a midgut where food can be stored.

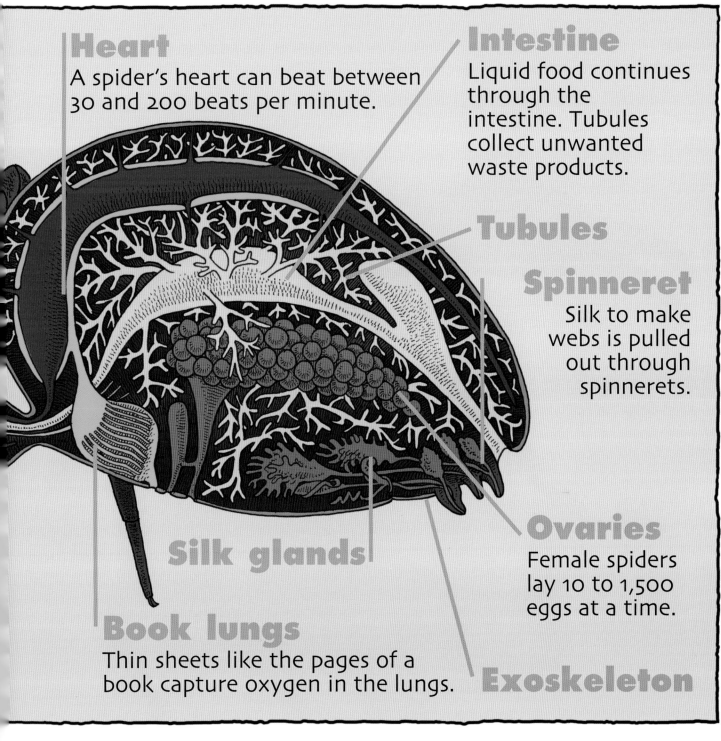

Heart
A spider's heart can beat between 30 and 200 beats per minute.

Intestine
Liquid food continues through the intestine. Tubules collect unwanted waste products.

Tubules

Spinneret
Silk to make webs is pulled out through spinnerets.

Silk glands

Ovaries
Female spiders lay 10 to 1,500 eggs at a time.

Book lungs
Thin sheets like the pages of a book capture oxygen in the lungs.

Exoskeleton

A female scorpion gives birth to live young. She looks after them for up to three weeks while they ride on her back.

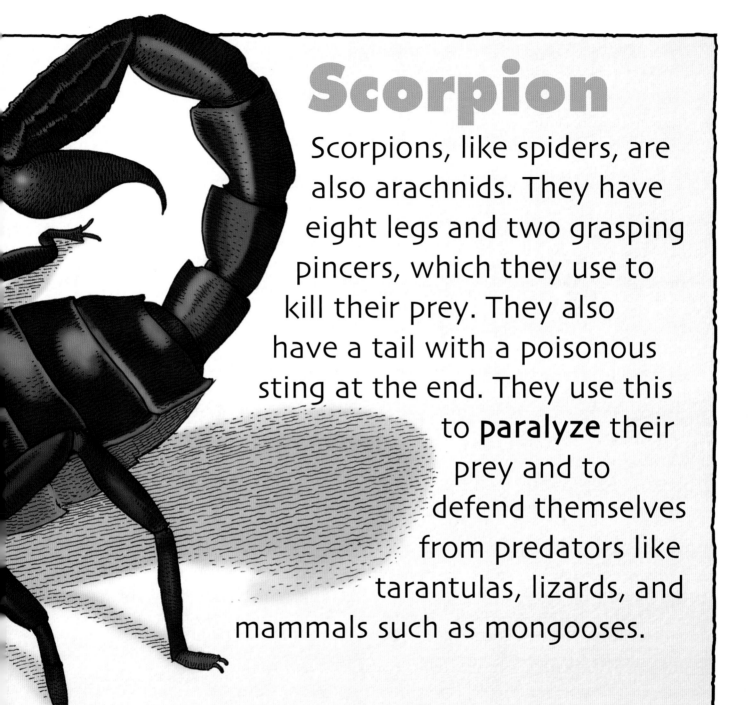

Scorpion

Scorpions, like spiders, are also arachnids. They have eight legs and two grasping pincers, which they use to kill their prey. They also have a tail with a poisonous sting at the end. They use this to **paralyze** their prey and to defend themselves from predators like tarantulas, lizards, and mammals such as mongooses.

Inside a **Scorpion**

Pincers

Scorpions use these to grab their prey of insects, spiders, and other scorpions.

Eyes

Scorpions have two main eyes on top and two sets of smaller eyes at the side.

Exoskeleton

Mouth

The small pincer-like mouth parts tear up the food.

Nerves and brain

The nervous system sends information about its surroundings to its brain .

Pectines

A pair of feathery structures detect vibrations on the ground.

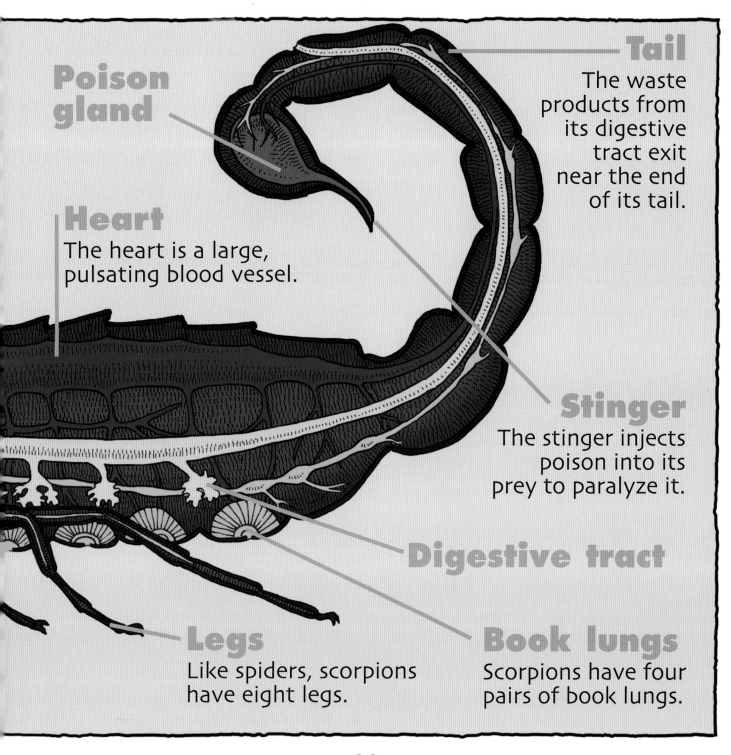

Poison gland

Tail
The waste products from its digestive tract exit near the end of its tail.

Heart
The heart is a large, pulsating blood vessel.

Stinger
The stinger injects poison into its prey to paralyze it.

Digestive tract

Legs
Like spiders, scorpions have eight legs.

Book lungs
Scorpions have four pairs of book lungs.

Glossary

colony An ant's nest.

nectar A sugar-rich liquid produced by plants.

nutrients Stuff from food that is essential for life and growth.

paralyze To make powerless and unable to move.

proboscis The elongated, sucking mouth part of an insect.

regurgitate To bring swallowed food back up to the mouth.

venom A form of poison used by an animal to paralyze or kill other animals.

Index